CREATIVE BEING

A Conversation with Gérome Barry

Heather Sanderson

Majestic Wisdom Publishing

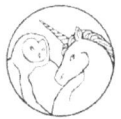

CONTENTS

PREFACE

When I started the Majestic Wisdom podcast in October 2020, I had no intention of turning the episodes into short books. I wanted to share conversations that I had with friends, teachers, and people I met who influenced and inspired me, so that others could also hear them. Having never listened to a podcast, and with very little sound editing experience, I set out to learn along the way. What I learned most is how much I love listening to people as they drop into the vulnerability of their heart, sharing openly and authentically from that place. It's truly beautiful.

We each have wisdom to share, and, from the outset, the goal of the podcast was to speak with people who, through their vision, dreams, passion, work, and creativity, embody wise ways of being for modern living. The process is very organic. People I know well, or have just met, will spark a feeling of resonance and light in my heart, and I'll ask if they're interested in co-creating an episode. Rarely, people I've never met reach out, their presence and magic nudging us into a collaboration.

About eight months after launching the podcast, I felt the energy of an idea floating around me: to turn the first podcast episode with Stewart Hoyt into a book. Unsure, I listed out all the complicating factors as to why this shouldn't be: getting permission from the collaborators, figuring out royalties, and the big one—how could I make the conversation work as a book? I placed enough hurdles in the way to talk myself out of trying. The idea popped up every so often and I brushed it aside until, in February 2022, the thought of making a book resurfaced again. This time with more intensity. This time I acquiesced and said yes, realizing that there are so many great thoughts and perspectives communicated in the podcasts, and they wanted to be shared with more people in another form!

So, here we are! (Now on book five of the series which I've called "The Future is Possible"). The process of creating that first book from a conversation was a brand-new, creative experience for me, and one that has been surprisingly engaging, exciting, and even overstimulating! Once the audio was transcribed into Word, it was fascinating to see patterns of speech on the page. The "if, if, ifs," and "you knows," and half formed sentences, trailing off into...

While leaving the words and integrity of the speaker's voice intact, I focused with great care on editing the conversation. Removing idioms, expressions, repetitions, and the attempts at formulating an idea three or four times before it emerges, fully formed, reminded me of removing the husk from a cob of corn. As the layers and patterns of speech were peeled back and away, a beautiful, nourishing, whole kernel of wisdom and truth was revealed. This process cracked open new ways of thinking about language; how different writing is to speaking, and the different expectations of a listener to those of a reader.

Listeners, in general, are more able to accept those quirks of speaking that each of us has, whereas readers tend to need more compliance to the rules of grammar and concision that are hard to accomplish in a conversation. This further emphasized the question: how will this work as a book? Only now, instead of dismissing the idea or quitting, it became a mission—one that has been highly generative and productive in the best possible ways.

Engaged by the problem-solving quest, answers kept coming on how to make this work. Once the conversation was cleaned up, so many options emerged in the form of structure. This was basic at first, like adding chapter headings, a question or two to break up longer soliloquies, and then expanded to creating additional pieces that don't exist in the podcast: this preface, the introduction, key concepts, footnotes, ways to inspire readers to engage with the conversation in the form of worksheets and synthesizing it all together in conclusion. Turns out,

I committed to taking one thing and helping it transform into something new. I am grateful to be the midwife of this rebirth, and I hope that within these pages you also find something transformative.

INTRODUCTION

I was "nomadic" at the time—living from place to place by choice with no fixed address. A transient existence meant I wasn't always able to connect in person regularly with friends in New York (where I had lived for six years before this life change) or attend events because I was in another town, in transit, or adjusting to a new location and didn't have the energy (or proximity) to attend. This is partly why November 30th, 2018 has a particular resonance for me.

Nineteen months (and ninety-five places) into my nomadic journey, I found myself on the Upper East Side, staying with my friend Mary. It was a Friday night and, every Friday back then, there was a wonderful swing dance event in Williamsburg, Brooklyn called Brooklyn Swings. Even when I had a place to live, getting to Williamsburg always felt like an ordeal. It took about an hour on transit, so I prioritized going on the one night a month when there was live music. A band gave me the extra push I needed to get out the door.

On the night I stayed with Mary, there wasn't meant to be a band, and the trek was just as far from her place as it was from my old one, but my friend Seth Harris was displaying his paintings and I wanted to see them and to be supportive. There was something else too—something I couldn't discern at the time, but it felt like a magnet, drawing me to the dance. Mary was up for it too, so we trundled off to the Q train, transferring to the L at 14th Street to Metropolitan Ave and wound our way to the church on Ainslie Street, where the dances had been held for years. I loved the venue—an off-the-main-road-hidden-away building which contributed to an underground feeling that I associate with swing dance.

Swing dance is a group of dances that originated in the Black community of Harlem, New York from the 1920s to 1940s, but my introduction to this style of dance was in the 1990s when I saw the film *Swing Kids*. From the moment I saw that film, all I wanted to do was dance like the people in it. As a non-dancer at the time, this felt like an impossibility. This is why every time I went to Brooklyn Swings, my heart widened as I saw the chairs stacked to the side of the room and the spacious wooden floor; twenty years after I watched *Swing Kids,* I *was* a dancer! Each time I entered the space, and heard the music, bliss stirred from so deep within me that I couldn't move fast enough to toss my coat onto the chairs, change my shoes, and find a partner. On this cold November night, I felt that same eagerness, yet I also sensed something different from previous times.

There was a gigantic, slow, invisible swirl moving overhead. Whatever it was, it felt supportive, uplifting, and energizing. I responded in kind, my energy and spirit lifted. Then came an announcement that not only would there be a surprise band, but someone was there filming the dance for a movie! The magic of the night continued as every single friend I had ever met on the dance floor was pulled there too, many of us after a long hiatus. These reunions added joy to the swirl and, as we all danced to the music, surrounded by Seth's gorgeous oil paintings of dancers and people dressed in 1940s attire, the film crew weaved its way through the authentic expression of community and camaraderie that social dancing can generate. The invisible swirl swelled above and around us and grew stronger until it became palpable: it was the spirit of the film. A creative being in its own right, the film collaborated with us and through us, feeding us and being fed.

The dance wound down by ten p.m. and, after Mary and I changed back into our street shoes and donned our coats, we chatted with some of the actors and crew. When we left, we were filled with the exuberance of the night; it bubbled through my cells so much that I wanted to know more about the film. What was this mysterious being? This energy?

We clattered through Mary's apartment door, and I flopped onto the couch, flipped open my laptop, and searched: "film Swing Rendez-vous."

My quest ended in seconds with the result of a crowd-funding website which included information about Gérome (the filmmaker), a synopsis of the film that I adored immediately (and you will hear about in our conversation), a trailer for fundraising and, way down at the bottom of the page there was an option to become an associate producer. My heart responded immediately to this call—it fluttered with enthusiasm and a desire to offer support. It was selfish, really, I wanted to participate in some way to ensure that the film came into the world and, even if it didn't, to have a way of saying "I love what you are doing here, how can I show you that?" I immediately sent Gérome an email to learn more about this possibility.

By the next day, Gérome and I had plans to meet and, when we did, we shared an inspiring conversation much like the one you are about to read. The conversation that follows took place two years later, in late November of 2020, when we were in the height of the pandemic. The film, *Swing Rendez-vous*, was almost complete right as the world (and theaters) shut down. Gérome talks about what that meant for him and shares the story and process of making the film from inception through to this pause. We talk about what creations came from his time in confinement in Paris, what it means to create within constrictions, and the paradigm of failure/success within the context of bringing a creation that has been stirring within you out into the world. What are the fears? The supports? How do you navigate them or draw upon them? What are the driving forces of creativity? Gérome sheds light on these questions, his process of gathering feedback, collaboration, and more as he shares his journey, motivation, and influences.

Part of our conversation includes a plant spirit reading, offered by me. In this case, it's a plant whose energy and spirit wanted to support Gérome and the creative process. A plant ally is a guide or friend who works on all levels: physically, spiritually, and energetically to assist in some way. The plants come to me intuitively, thanks to years of training in Sacred Plant Medicine with Carole Guyett, and by being open to connecting with them. I often feel their energy around me or see an image of the plant in my mind's eye when they want to share some information. Including the plants in the conversation in this way helps get out of the human-centric mindset many of us carry, helps rebalance the relationship between plants and humans, and adds another layer of inquiry and support. This may be a new concept for some, and I invite and encourage you to stay open to the possibility that humans and plants can co-create together on many levels.

As you read, consider make notes for your own self-reflection and listen to your own creative impulses. Creativity can often be rigidly defined, repressed, shut down, or be countered with inner voices of self-doubt. It can, of course, also flourish and creative projects may flow through you with ease. Notice any emotions that surface and, if you feel safe to do so, put the book down and sit with or feel those emotions. You don't need to identify what they are, just see what energy is moving within the structure that is you. This is a great way to learn what is "you" and what is not; a stepping stone to discern what the energy of creativity feels like in your body.

To that end, you might also feel into your heart —what sensations are there as you read different sections of this book? Do some feelings need to be nurtured or explored further? Do any creative projects or expressions ask for your attention? If they do, can you write them down without dismissing them? And, as always, take the parts of this book that resonate for you and leave the rest.

CREATIVE BEING

Now that you have the background and context, I'd like to welcome you into the conversation with Gérome Barry. As you read our exchange, notice any times when you feel inspired, called to create, doubtful, hopeful, sad, joyful, or any other emotion that rises within you. I invite you to consider these emotions, thoughts, and any new ideas that emerge, so that you can continue the conversation in your own way once you've finished this book. You will also find some key concepts at the end of the book to further enhance your exploration.

The Origins Of *Swing Rendez-Vous*

HEATHER SANDERSON: I'm here today with independent filmmaker and creative soul Gérome Barry.

GÉROME BARRY: Hello, thank you.

HS: Thanks for joining us from Paris, France! Let's dive right in! You and I met in Brooklyn, NY when you were working on the feature film, Swing Rendez-vous. Can you share a little bit about how that film started for you?

GB: Yes—it all started in 2017—that is to say, the very first idea for it happened then. I hadn't been to New York for about ten years, but I do have French friends who live in New York, and they kept telling me, "You should come and see us."

They are musicians there. They play jazz and they invited me a lot and then finally, after all those years, I decided to go and see them and I discovered the jazz world, with Lindy Hop dancers and swing dancing and a music environment which is very old fashioned. I discovered all that and I thought it would be a great topic for a movie and a great community to shoot.

HS: I love it. I love it because you found this other world in New York.

GB: That's true because all those places are kind of underground places. Not everybody knows them. And that's really something I wanted to show to the whole world. Because they deserve it. The musician's life is something extraordinary. I mean literally, it's out of any ordinary life, and it's really something I wanted to show. So, we started to build our story together—my friends and I. That's how it all started.

HS: Beautiful. So, it was very collaborative.

GB: Yes—it's all based on real stories and most of it is based on real events, although nobody can guess that by watching the film itself because we managed to build an actual plot. It's all about romance, which is pure fiction. But everything else is true.

HS: It sounds like you came to New York, entered this other world, and were inspired. Was filmmaking something you were already doing? Or were you working on something else at the time? I guess the question is: how did making the film start after you had the idea?

GB: When I first came to New York, I was invited by my friends. The days I spent there were just holidays. I didn't expect anything to be honest. I was working full-time in film production, and I had been doing that for four years. I had also directed a few short films, but I can't say that I really expected to get involved in such a such a project, just after spending a few weeks in New York, but that's what happened. I decided to quit my job a few months later and that was a big step, trust me.

HS: How did that feel?

GB: Well, I have to be honest; I felt like that was a relief and that I was finally doing what I wanted to do, but it was very scary at the same time. I loved, and still love film production and I'm still doing that in a way. Film production and film direction are two different things, but I love them both, so getting involved in this project felt very natural to me, but very scary.

One day I would feel enthusiastic and the next day,

I'd wonder, "What am I doing? What am I doing here? It's just a nightmare." And that's it. It's been like that for three years.

HS: It sounds like you stepped into a lot of unexpected things. How the idea for the film came was very organic and you went with it, even though you were terrified a lot of the time.

GB: Now the project is almost done so I can confess that some moments were very tough, yes. But I really had that goal of making the film in mind and there was no way I would fail or not go to the end of it. No way. I never had any doubt about that. From the second I started it.

Finding An Audience

HS: That's amazing, to have that amount of confidence and focus.

GB: I wouldn't say confidence. Confidence is part of it, for sure, but it's just the strong will I had to go to the end of that journey.

I wasn't ready to stop before the end, simply because I wanted to see that movie. It's literally as simple as that: I'm just making the film I want to see.

HS: To see and to show other people?

GB: Yes, of course, but I have to be the first audience.

HS: I like that. And when you started to see it develop and maybe even watched it for the first time, what was that experience like for you?

GB: Wow, that's a really tough question.

HS: Only if you feel comfortable sharing, take a minute.

GB: It's just that there were so many first times. Because there were so many times when I thought the film was there, but it wasn't. And that's what film editing is all about.

It takes a lot of time, and you can never see the end of the process. It's endless; you can spend your life editing a movie and at some point, you need to stop. I never stopped until I thought the film was good enough, but that took months and months.

HS: And when you were doing that, were you showing it to other people or getting feedback? How did you know it was closer to being finished?

GB: Yes, we showed our first versions to a lot of people. Some of them were aware of the project, but others were not, and they knew nothing about it because we wanted to have different opinions. All of them were very useful. All of them. But at one point, when you show one version to someone, and then a second version, and then the third version … at some point they understandably get annoyed, so you can't do that too many times.

Feedback is very important; it's crucial. At one point I had a revelation and felt that we needed something else. A few things came to my mind —obvious things that were missing. From that moment, I decided to set focus groups and do test screenings.

We did that in Paris and in New York with two different kinds of audiences; one French audience and one American audience. We did that very professionally with surveys, and precise questions and they had to rate the characters because I wanted to have a general idea of what the feeling was in the screening room, and I used all of that feedback. That was very, very useful and I kept improving the editing until last summer.

HS: I imagine that listening to what people had to say could sometimes be exciting and sometimes be challenging to receive.

How did you make decisions? How did you decide when to change something and when to leave it as is?

GB: That's very interesting. I don't know what to say about that. Intuition is very important, of course. When I was editing the film, I had my own intuition, but sometimes it's hard to put those feelings into words. So, to me, those tests and surveys and questions help me put words on what I was feeling in the first place.

HS: That makes a lot of sense.

GB: Yeah, it's all very natural. You can see very easily from the surveys who is the right audience for the movie and who is not. It's very easy.

Once you notice that someone could be interested

but found that certain elements were not good enough, you need to pay attention to it and do something. Of course, you can't change everything; that would be senseless. But everyone has something interesting to say. So that process was very, very useful.

It might sound like a marketing thing or something very professional and austere, but it's not. It's really not. It's just a way that that I've found to communicate with my possible audience. And it was a way for them to tell me things honestly and anonymously.

HS: And it all contributed to the final project that you're so close to finishing now. When it is complete and ready to be released to the world, what is it that you hope Swing Rendez-vous will bring to people?

GB: I'd say joy. Yeah, I'd say joy and a smile. That would be a great achievement for me if I could bring joy and a smile and maybe laughter to people—that would be great. I'll be very, very happy. And whether the film is good or not, I'm pretty sure that it has great music, so it can't be completely bad.

The Players

HS: Do you want to share a bit about the musicians and whose great music is in the film?

GB: Oh, I was very lucky because I've been working with a composer whose name is Giovanni Mirabassi.

He's a great jazz man, a great jazz piano player, and we've worked together on all of my films so far (my short movies and this feature film) and I feel very, very grateful and honored because he's such a great musician.

The idea is that I wanted to mix different atmospheres which all relate to jazz but are usually communities and people that don't really talk to each other, and what I really love is making films where I can make people from different environments and backgrounds meet each other.

Giovanni Mirabassi is a modern jazz composer and the music I was filming in New York is swing jazz and traditional jazz and I wanted to mix that, but also respect everyone. That's very important. So, Giovanni wrote jazz standards in the spirit of the swing standards from the 1930s. And the musicians would just play them live with their own style and I loved that. That is really the heart of the project and that's exactly what I wanted to shoot and what I wanted to record: the encounter of those two worlds which are so close to each other without even knowing it.

HS: That's really special and like a blending to create something new.

GB: Exactly. And the whole story is about a jazz standard, so that was exactly the point. It's all about a character looking for an old jazz standard.

HS: And going on an epic quest.

GB: Exactly.

HS: The music was recorded live. Who was playing the music? Who were the musicians involved?

GB: The musicians were my New York friends. The main singer is Tatiana Eva-Marie. She's an old friend of mine. We've been friends for years and years now and I really wanted to film her and record her music with my friend Adrien Chevalier, as well.

Those are my friends. I wanted to show their world and to film and record their music. I was so happy that they could be a part of the movie. The film is inspired by their lives. It's a tribute that I wanted to shoot and to make about them.

HS: These were the friends that you were first staying with when you were in New York?

GB: Oh yes. Not only staying with, but I followed them everywhere. They were playing every night and I was constantly discovering a new place. They showed me basically everything about the swing jazz scene in New York, which is really fascinating.

Yes, they were at the origin of the movie, and I had wanted to make a film or some kind of creative project with Tatiana and Adrien for a long time. This was the perfect occasion.

HS: And they also star in the film, correct?

GB: Yes, because basically the French cast is made of professional actors. For example, there was Estéban who's a young actor—a very funny actor. I love him.

He was really great. I also had cameos from very famous French people you might have heard of. One of them is Arielle Dombasle and the other one is Bernard Pivot. And last but not least, my fictional mother was played by Edwige Morgen, a fabulous jazz singer who is also a great actress.

That was for the French part of the film, but regarding the American part, I wanted the musicians to play their own parts on the big screen. I just asked them to be themselves, and that's what they did. And I was so happy and so proud of that. For example, I remember one or two sequences that were directly inspired by real events and real facts and stories and things that I had seen and lines of dialogue that I had heard between them, and I wanted to recreate that.

When I managed to do it, that was such a joy for me. I truly brought what I had witnessed to the screen and that was fabulous. I love that and I won't tell you what sequences they are—it's all a surprise, but I'm very proud of them and I managed to bring almost the same people to the same places with the same lines of dialogue and recreate that. And it feels so natural and it's also part of a fictional section of the plot. I'm very proud of that.

HS: What I hear in your description is that you were inclusive in working with the people who were there from the very start. Making sure they were involved the whole time.

GB: Yes, that's very important to me. I really need the

crew I work with to be involved in the project and not just do it because they're forced to and not because of the money, obviously. We had almost no money; just enough to make it possible, but nothing more.

Creativity From Confinement

HS: Changing focus a little bit. So, we have this character's epic quest in Swing Rendez-vous going between Paris and New York. And the reality is that you've been in Paris yourself, in confinement, for much of this year.

GB: Like a lot of people, I guess.

HS: Like a lot of people. But from that, I'm curious if you could share with us: who is Colin? And what has Colin been up to during confinement?

GB: Oh! Colin is a character I created without even thinking about it. When it started, I think it was good for me to take a short break from *Swing Rendez-vous*. Because you sometimes need time to get new ideas for the editing. It's such a long process. So, I used that confinement time to do something else and I started to make short movies, like little jokes.

At first it was very simple. I didn't even think about it. I never wrote anything. I just took my iPhone and started to shoot very simple things in my living room and bedroom and then I noticed that people liked it, so I kept doing them.

It's such a funny story. The first video took me five

hours in total. I woke up in the morning and I didn't even know that I would shoot anything that day but, after I created it and posted it on YouTube and social media, all of a sudden it was shared hundreds of times. So, the next ones took me longer: one day, then two days, then three days, then more and more.

HS: Getting more and more involved.

GB: Yes.

HS: And a few of these have also been noticed by different film festivals.

GB: That's true.

HS: That's exciting, congratulations!

GB: Crazily enough, yes, thank you. Yeah, that's very strange to me, but yes. I think for the moment, twenty or twenty-five festivals have selected it, which is crazy, and we won a few prizes as well. My little films went to Australia and Argentina, India, Greece, the US. A lot of festivals in the US ... not Canada, not yet.

HS: I'm surprised! I'll work on that!

GB: Maybe they will. Thank you for that.

HS: I love it. It's like there's this organic process that unfolded and is flowing through you and you're able to go with it in a way, to have that inspiration and intuition, and then release it. Put it into the world, see what happens. That's so inspiring to me.

GB: Well, again, I didn't even think about it when I made the first one. I woke up in the morning and I had no idea that I will be doing that that day.

The beginning of the confinement was, like for so many people, depressing and scary and I didn't know what to do. I was a bit lost. I was still editing my film and stuck at my place, so at one point I decided to break all that and do something. That's it.

HS: And shift the energy.

GB: Yes, and that experience actually helped me for the editing process of the feature film.

HS: How so?

GB: For example, I drew and animated a few sequences for my short confinement videos, which is something I hadn't done for years. I mean, I hadn't drawn anything for years. So, I got back to that and noticed it was very successful and it was also a way to convey things in a funny way and to create new environments and a new perspective, so I decided to add short animated sequences to my feature film. That way of expressing myself is slowly becoming a part of my work now.

HS: And maybe you never would have come across it again if it hadn't been for this time in confinement.

GB: Never! Without the confinement period, I'm absolutely sure that I wouldn't have thought about adding animated sequences to *Swing Rendez-vous*. Never. So, confinement brought that idea to me, strangely enough.

HS: I think there's something to be said about creating within constriction or constraints. They are a really good motivator for invention. In this case, you had to figure out, when you just had your apartment and yourself, what is it that you are going to do with the situation?

GB: Well … if I can't film something I just need to draw it. It's as simple as that. That's absolutely true. I think creation gets its roots out of restrictions. Complete freedom is scary; what can you do with complete creation freedom? It's too large. You can't do anything, and what's the point? I mean, what's the context? What do you do? What do you have inside yourself that you can express freely without any context or audience or anything? That's really hard. Every creation is part of the context, so the context is more important than we think.

HS: And I feel like Colin is really showing that.

GB: Hopefully. I tried my best.

HS: You did great.

GB: It also reminds me of *Monty Python and The Holy Grail*. It might sound strange because what I do has nothing to do with them, but they are a great influence, not only because they are geniuses, but also because when they were doing the *Holy Grail*, they had no money. I mean, they did everything with the equivalent of, I think, €300,000 today.[1]

HS: That's why the horses are coconuts?

GB: Yes, of course, because if they didn't have that kind of budget restriction, would they have even thought of bringing in the coconuts?

HS: Probably not.

GB: And that's why the movie is so funny. That's why it's still a masterpiece.

HS: You're helping me realize it's true in life; you need to work with what you have. And follow it through to some end or some purpose and then return and try again. You keep repeating and uncovering even more.

GB: Yes, because that's part of one's story. One life can't be summed up with only the successes. The path towards those successes is as interesting and maybe even more interesting. I'm more and more convinced about that idea.

HS: That's where the riches are.

GB: Yes, absolutely.

Plant Spirit Reading

HS: As part of the conversation, I want to offer a plant spirit reading for you.

GB: OK.

HS: This can be many different things. Generally, it's a plant that has come forward to work or collaborate with you in some way. What I mean by that is, I ask to be shown a plant that wants to connect with you, and I see it as an image in my mind. It could be a plant that embodies the energy you're already working with. It could be a plant that wants you to have tea with it every day for a little while. It could have any meaning whatsoever that you apply.

Are you curious?

GB: I have one in mind but let let's see.

HS: I wonder if we have the same one. The plant that has appeared for you is Rosemary.

GB: Interesting …

HS: I'll tell you a bit about her, and then I want to hear the plant that you're thinking of.

GB: Yeah, you'll see why I'm saying it's interesting when you know mine.

HS: I'm intrigued! Rosemary is a very fiery plant. She offers humans lot of energy and a lot of focus. Rosemary tea can replace coffee, for example, because there's so much energy that can move through you with Rosemary and she's usually very energizing.

GB: Oh wow, I didn't know that.

HS: She also helps with inspiration and having the steady internal fire to carry things through to the end, like a big project for example. Not only the initiating force but also the sustaining energy. She keeps your personal fire balanced and stoked.

The thing about Rosemary that I also like is that she's

often associated with birth. In this sense, the process that you've been going through is a creative birth in many ways. You stepped out of an old life—a job and a structure that you were used to—and into an unknown world so that you could create something that's moving through you. Then bring that creative being—which is part of you as you are a creative being yourself and yet is also its own separate entity—into the world. That's why I like Rosemary for you. Any thoughts on that?

GB: Well, that's very interesting. I guess it describes me quite well. That's very informative too because I had no idea you could drink Rosemary instead of coffee.

HS: Hearing you say that is prompting me to say Rosemary has lots of benefits. She also helps with memory and helps with blood flow.

GB: I should drink liters of that. I have a very bad memory. Memory like a goldfish.

HS: There you go. Maybe that's why she's coming up for you.

GB: It's good to know. Regarding the creative process, I recently realized that the moments in my life when I feel the happiest is when I create things. Creating things is my deepest motivation. Every day I need to create; I need to be in the process of making things. Making things is what makes me happy.

HS: That's amazing and it's so interesting because fire and creativity are often linked as well. Rosemary can support you in making things in your creative endeavors.

GB: Yes!

HS: She might be a plant for you to work with more if you want to explore her.

GB: I will. And you know what plant I was thinking about?

HS: I want to hear.

GB: It's very funny because I was thinking about Thyme.

HS: Wow!

GB: Thyme, which is very close, isn't it?

HS: Very close.

GB: Usually they come from the same climate or region. I come from the South of France in Provence, and you can find Rosemary and Thyme and similar plants growing there. It's also funny because they are both parts of the same song. Do you know *Scarborough Fair*?

HS: I do, and I was just thinking of that!

GB: "*Parsley, Sage, Rosemary, and Thyme. Are you going to Scarborough Fair?*" It's very funny because that was close.

HS: And together they're musical plants. You just sang the song with them.

GB: Oh, yes, because of the song.

HS: Maybe they can be stars in your next film.

GB: I'll definitely think about it.

HS: But you're right, they're so linked! I love that Thyme came to your mind.

GB: Yeah, it's the first thing that came to my mind. I also love the smell of Rosemary.

HS: Maybe you can make a Rosemary and Thyme tea by combining them together—that would be delicious.

GB: Yes, I do that sometimes to be honest.

HS: You're already on it—great! That makes me happy.

Gérome's Work

HS: Where can people find out more about Swing Rendez-vous and the confinement films you've been doing?

GB: The easiest way is to follow me on social media. I'm on Instagram and Facebook, but mainly Instagram. People can look for my name (@geromebarry) on Instagram and I'll be more than happy to share what I do every day with them. I think that's the best way to get connected.

HS: Thank you so much for that information. And thank you for sharing so much of your story. I really appreciate it.

GB: It was my pleasure. Thank you. Thank you so much.

CONCLUSION

T hat November night at Brooklyn Swings, I met the film before I knew anything about it. I felt it in the room. I saw its energy rotating overhead, moving with us and through us as we danced. This is why, for me, the film is a creative being of its own. You might think of it as a force that accompanied, or is the essence of, the film. The ideas for it came from Gérome and from his community of friends—and perhaps those seeds of ideas are what first sparked the spirit of Swing Rendez-vous to be conceived. Or perhaps the film and its story existed in some unconscious state or place, external or internal to the people involved, seemingly invisible and waiting to be accessed and given form. Who am I to know? It doesn't matter which is true, because the reality is that any creative endeavor is a collaboration and co-creation in a multitude of ways and almost always includes an inherent element of mystery. A dance with the unknown.

This dance and ability to co-create with these seemingly invisible forces is always present.

Creativity comes from within us as well as outside of us, and everyone has access to it with it, whether or not they are aware. Finding it may not always feel possible, and it can take practice to learn your own ways of connecting with and listening to the creative beings which want to emerge through you. When Gérome said that he had to create something every day, it struck a chord of resonance deep in my heart. A knowing that not only is this true but it is also a necessity of life (not a luxury as creativity is often viewed). There is some motivating force inherent to creativity and, at the same time, it is an energy that feeds us. A daily practice is also a way to learn your ways of listening and accessing this energy.

A daily creation doesn't have to be a short film or a painting or any artifact you associate with a "creative art," it can be preparing a new meal, taking a picture on your phone, moving your body in a new way, forming and/or deepening relationships, or walking a different route than you normally do. Our thoughts, feelings, decisions, the way we organize a day, problem-solve, how we move through both pleasurable and stressful situations or crisis are all creative impulses. What we can do with what we have, within constrictions and constraints, to form something new again and again and again.

Creativity is constant, fluid, and always in motion. Perhaps this is why it can feel elusive. Especially if you think creativity must look or be a certain way. It doesn't.

Often the doubt and worry about doing something creative stem from some form of internalized measurement and worthiness which can be protective or can hold you, and your creative energy, back. As if to create is to risk yourself whereas I venture that to create, especially with authenticity, means tending to yourself. It's an opportunity to explore your inner world and express it to the outer world. No one ever needs to see it unless you choose to share it. If you do, trust your audience, or find one to trust. Gérome's process of soliciting and receiving feedback reminds me that it's not always easy to open up to others but, when you do, the audience and support will be there. The collaborative energy which runs through all of *Swing Rendez-vous* makes it stronger than it would have been if developed in isolation.

Spoiler alert: fast forward two more years from the time of this conversation and *Swing Rendez-vous* has launched into the world—with a premier in Paris on December 6th, 2022. I like to believe that the film was waiting for the right time to emerge. Its spirit trusting in the alignment that would come. Waiting and patience take courage and are not always easy to trust in, especially when you want to complete a process or have the being you have been working with, and possibly even loving, be birthed.

As Gérome said, he wanted this film to bring joy to people and, as we continue to process the global pandemic both individually and collectively, I couldn't imagine a better time for an infusion of levity and happiness. Now that it's out in the world, there is a freedom that accompanies this phase of being: the creator lets go and the film is its own entity on its own independent journey. There is no control over what happens next. Who knows what people will receive from it, what or how it will impact others or their creations, the relationships it will have, or where it will go next? Likely this is beyond comprehension—and I feel a radiant glow in my heart as I imagine the ripples and reach of *Swing Rendez-vous,* because it is unknowable. That is part of the magic.

OVER TO YOU

Feel inspired? Want to explore your creativity, make a commitment to a daily practice, or move through creative blocks? Try the exercises on the following pages to explore these concepts further. See what comes to the surface for you in this moment and use the space on the pages to draw or write what comes. Your answers may change over time.

CREATIVITY

Do you think of yourself as a creative being? Whether your answer is "yes" or "no," use this page to write down all the ways in which you are, ever have been, and/or want to be creative.

DEVELOPING A PRACTICE

We all create something every day. Even if it's the schedule of how the day will unfold. I invite you to choose one "creative art" and set an amount of time to try it out for a week or a month. See what happens. Record observations here if you so choose.

CREATIVE BELIEF BLOCKS

Write out a list of all the things that stop you from being "creative" or creating your life how you want it to be. The voices you have heard from others, and your own. Look at them to see if there is one belief that stands out. An example of this could be "I'm not good enough." Then, write down the opposite belief or beliefs. Repeat these opposite statements to yourself.

CONSTRAINTS

To help connect or play with your creativity, try a constraint. For example, turn to three pages in this book and choose the first three words that call your attention. Then, use this page to write a poem or story about them, dance the words, draw them, or play some notes on an instrument that the words inspire.

CONNECTING WITH A CREATIVE PROJECT

This can occur in many ways. Perhaps in the shower or when you are out walking, you will have a flash of an idea. Write it down or record it in some way. You may also sit quietly, meditate, or dream, and ask to meet a creative project/creativity itself. Trust what happens. Once you sense/hear/see this being, spend some time together. Ask questions. Record the answers. Develop a relationship with this being and keep checking back in as often as you choose.

COMMITMENT

Make one commitment to yourself for a creative practice or project that you will put into action.

My commitment is to: _____

KEY CONCEPTS

Some of the concepts in this conversation may be new to you, can't be found in the dictionary, or are meant differently than the definitions you'll find there or in a Google search. Words, language, and definitions evolve as humans explore and experiment, which is an essential part of shifting how we live, create, and envision ourselves and the world around us. With this context in mind, here are a few terms that may be of interest. You may have additional interpretations to add to these concepts, too.

Constraints/Constriction

The terms constraint and constriction are slightly different in their definitions. A constraint means a limitation or restriction whereas a constriction means the action to make something narrower by pressure, tightening, or an obstruction.

When I think of working within constraints it conjures up project management jargon of a "triple constraint." In business projects, at least, this means that a project is always being monitored and controlled in relation to the constraints of time, money, and scope (goal upon completion). Imagine these three things as interrelated so when one changes, the others are also impacted and need to change. For example, if money is not a concern and you are running out of time, you might add more people to a project to complete it by a deadline, or you might change the scope of what needs to be accomplished (thus redefining the outcome of the project).

Any of these constraints can feel like pressure and tightening in the physical body of the people working on the project. Being with and moving through that energy is also part of the process. When does pressure or a tightening in the body aid you in working on a project, and when do these sensations need to be alleviated? The answer to that question often also impacts the output. People and projects are not separate but are always working in a co-creative process. Keep this relationship in mind as you continue to read about constraints in relation to the creative process because what you feel as a creator is important. The context, background, and privilege that surround a project (and the life of the creator) are also important to recognize and are major influences when it comes to constraint, constriction, and pressure in relation to creativity, as are the beliefs of an individual, group, culture, and society.

A constraint, when it comes to creative work, may be related to this concept of a triple constraint as well—when money is tight it can foster a need for problem-solving or a different approach, thus altering the final outcome that is produced. You may have a zero-dollar budget (as I do for my books!) and instead exchange services for the time and skill of others if you need their help on a project, or for resources you need in order to create. If you can't buy a canvas and paint, for example, you might volunteer at a local art school in exchange for using their tools.

Time, too, can be worked with as a constraint. You might set a limit (or timer) for how long you will write, draw, paint, dance, film, photograph, write music, sculpt, etc. It could be a short five-minute burst, or an hour. The pressure of a limited timeframe will generate a different result than if time extended on forever. Endless time often creates inertia or a malaise that you will "do it someday." Time could also mean going on a retreat (whether it be for a day or a month) and allowing yourself time to dream and be creative in some way. Adding a timeframe around what you are doing creates a container within which to play and discover.

Working within constraints or constrictions can also mean intentionally creating an obstacle or limitation as part of the creative process. There are many ways to do this. One way most people have experience with is cooking: making a recipe out of items left in the cupboard that you may not normally put together. Another common example is that of a haiku poem. This is an unrhymed poetic form consisting of 17 syllables arranged in three lines of 5, 7, and 5 syllables, respectively.[2] When you need to work within a set number of syllables for each line, the end result will be different than if you were writing all of your thoughts in a journal. The constraint pushes you to think within a container.

Often this container is part of the challenge and encourages you to do something out of the ordinary; it mixes things up. This helps support the growth of new connections and pathways in the brain and often leads to innovative creations that you would never have generated otherwise. Without a constraint, there would be no need to think differently. This can be as simple as learning a new dance step (even if you are a non-dancer) to deciding to take a different photo of a dog, cat, leaf, plant, sky (anything!) every day in a different place or context. In this case, the act of repetition challenges you to create something unique and/or to study something in depth, and to pay attention to details in different ways—what stays the same and what changes?

The OuLiPo (short for *Ouvroir de littérature potentielle*), founded in 1960 by a group of mathematicians and writers set out to write within constraints and they offer many ideas for how to do this. The group roughly defines the term *littérature potentielle* as: "the seeking of new structures and patterns which may be used by writers in any way they enjoy."[3] Some of their techniques include writing a poem and then replacing every noun with the seventh noun after its position in a dictionary. See what you get! Or writing a story without using one or more letters. The Brooklyn Public Library and the Writhing Society host a workshop to explore these and other OuLiPo-inspired constraints such as using a random emoji-generator and writing a poem that includes all the images or only using words from a fairy tale to make something new.

It's like a game and brings a problem-solving approach (and perhaps some pressure) to, in this case, the writing process and you can extrapolate the essence of this to any creative endeavor. The outcome isn't necessarily as important as the act of creation and the internal shifts that accompany experimentation. Working within constraints sets a safe foundation for creative expansion and growth.

Creativity

Creativity is a concept that expands beyond many of the typical definitions for it. *Encyclopedia Britannica* defines creativity as "the ability to make or otherwise bring into existence something new, whether a new solution to a problem, a new method or device, or a new artistic object or form." This is entirely true, and, like many definitions is human-centric. Everything is creation and is constantly in a cycle of birth/life/

death/repeat. This includes plants, animals, land, and all of life that plays out in each moment. To think of creativity as a purely human act is to see through a narrow and limiting lens. This lens tends to generate beliefs that people are either creative or not. That you either have it or you don't.

Many people see themselves as impostors if an idea hasn't come purely from them or if they aren't sure where it came from. This mindset excludes a crucial part of the process: co-creation. Whether you use the word spirit, muse, energy, inspiration, consciousness, or any of the many other ways to describe it, creativity is always a multi-dimensional experience (of the physical world and of another). The process of co-creation sometimes requires action, sometimes surrender and always learning how to listen; listening to yourself, your intuition, the guidance and collaboration of other humans (when it resonates with you), and to that other contributing force—the creative being that wants to work through you in some way.

Creative Freedom

The word freedom means different things to each individual and is highly dependent upon the culture and context from which you come and/or in which you live. According to UNESCO, artistic freedom is "the freedom to imagine, create and distribute diverse cultural expressions free of governmental censorship, political interference, or the pressures of non-state actors. It includes the right of all citizens to have access to these works and is essential for the wellbeing of societies." This kind of freedom is one to which not all humans have safe access.

Creative freedom and "freedom of expression," in Western (or at least American) culture is often defined as the ability to make, do, or say whatever you want. This conversation has me wondering about another kind of creative freedom: letting go of the outcome. What comes from the freedom to create without expectation that what you are making or doing will turn into anything, lead anywhere, be "good," easy, hard, or any other assumptions you carry in this regard. Even with *Swing Rendez-vous*, there were no guarantees that the film would ever be distributed; yet it wanted to exist.

Plant Spirit

The concept of a plant spirit is difficult to put into words because it can be experienced in so many different ways. To me, plant spirits are the consciousness and essence of a plant—that which is embodied in its physical form and exists around and outside of the physical body as energy and/or vibration. The spirit of a plant may also exist without a physical presence.

Think of your own spirit. What does the word 'spirit' mean for you? Maybe you think of spirit as the energy or quality which animates your body, a vibration in your heart, the part of you that connects to some larger energy or life force. Beyond the energy of the physical plant, its spirit has the ability to move and be moved, and to communicate in many ways that we can see, hear, feel, or sense in some way (and often ignore). Connecting with a plant is important because you can gain a sense of what spirit means for you, and how to work with plants individually and collectively.[4]

ENDNOTES

1. **Fun fact:** according to Wikipedia, a 2021 tweet by Eric Idle revealed that the film was financed by eight investors: **Led Zeppelin**, **Pink Floyd**, **Jethro Tull's Ian Anderson**, *Holy Grail*'s co-producer **Michael White**, Heartaches (a cricket team founded by lyricist **Tim Rice**), and three record companies including **Charisma Records**. The investors contributed the entire original budget of £175,350 (about $410,000 in 1974).

2. For more information on the history of haiku poetry and the evolution of constraints this form of poetry has undergone visit https://www.britannica.com/art/haiku.

3. To learn more about the history and practices of the OuLiPo visit https://en.wikipedia.org/wiki/Oulipo#cite_note-CB-11

4. This excerpt can be found in each of Heather's Plant and Tree Spirit Short Reads. For more, visit, www.majesticwisdompublishing.com/books

ACKNOWLEDGMENTS

A huge thank you to Gérome Barry for sharing his work, passion, integrity and for his constant support and friendship. I'm always grateful that *Swing Rendez-vous* brought us together! I'd also like to thank Vanja Adzovic for her keen editorial feedback and guidance on this, and on many other books and works in progress. Deanna McFadden for her constant encouragement and our daily exchange of voluminous text messages, ideas, and unwavering dedication to one another's work and to working with Dr. Clarissa Pinkola Estés Réyes and Carole Guyett who both taught me how to journey to and meet with a creative being, and to honor my own voice, in different ways. While writing this book, Dr. Pinkola Estés Réyes' words came through in particular, reminding me to create, put that creation out into the world, and repeat. Then repeat again. I have taken that to heart and her message to do so is inherent in why and how books exist.

Thanks to Erik Schurink who introduced me to

The Writhing Society and the OuLiPo. I also love how Rasa Morrison was able to take a messy sketch of a unicorn and an owl, representing majestic wisdom, scribbled on the back of a notebook and turn it into the beautiful logo and cover image you see here.

And, of course, with deepest respect and honor to the plants who truly are guiding it all.

ABOUT GÉROME

Gérome Barry studied political science before entering La Fémis cinema school in Paris. He produced about ten short films, which won awards at international festivals. Then he directed four short films: *The Big Musical Number* (musical comedy, audience award at Beijing film festival), *Séraphin* (dark comedy), *Suicide Express* (comedy, jury award at Montpellier film festival) and *Expedition Under My Bed* (55 festival selections and 5 awards around the world).

Meanwhile, he worked for many years in film production, first as a script consultant for Cinémage (French investment company) and Quad Cinema (producer of *The Intouchables*), and then as a post-production supervisor for Moby Dick Films (*Mademoiselle de Joncquières*), where he had the chance to work with directors such as Emmanuel Mouret, Jean Paul Civeyrac and Serge Avédikian.

His first feature film *Swing Rendez-vous*, a romantic and musical comedy à la Jacques Tati or Jacques Demy, was released on cinema screens in France in January 2023.

ABOUT HEATHER

Heather Sanderson has written 20+ plant and tree spirit short reads, a collection of poetry, short healing arts books, several podcast episodes, hundreds of yoga classes and workshops, Reiki trainings, and plant spirit offerings. Trained in many healing arts disciplines, she focuses on bringing her magic and medicine to the world and encourages others to do the same. You can find her books at www.majesticwisdompublishing.com, her other work at www.journeythroughyoga.com, and follow her on Instagram at @heather.sanderson.

ABOUT MAJESTIC WISDOM PODCAST

Majestic Wisdom podcast invites you to remember your magic and bring it into the world, whatever it may be. Learn from the wisdom of others, and all the different ways there are to live a life, to engage with the world, and to create. Each episode also features a plant spirit teaching inspired by the guest. To listen to an episode, visit www.majesticwisdompublishing.com/podcast.

BOOKS BY THIS AUTHOR

Plant Spirit Short Reads
Dreaming with Dandelion
Dreaming with Elder
Dreaming with Heather
Dreaming with Holly
Dreaming with Goldenrod
Dreaming with Mugwort
Dreaming with Nettle
Dreaming with Red Clover
Dreaming with Rhubarb
Dreaming with Rosemary
Dreaming with Sumac
Dreaming with Sunflower
Dreaming with Trillium
Dreaming with Violet

Tree Spirit Short Reads
Dreaming with Apple
Dreaming with Birch
Dreaming with Hawthorn
Dreaming with Oak
Dreaming with Redwood
Dreaming with Spruce
Dreaming with Willow

Healing Arts Short Reads
Loving Kindness for Everyday Life
Understanding Reiki
Yoga Nidra for Everyday Life

Poetry
Sister, (a collection of poems)

The Future is Possible Series
Building the Future Now Through Reiki: A Conversation with Nathalie Biermanns
Building the Future Now Through Yoga: A Conversation with Deanna Green
Creative Being: A Conversation with Gérome Barry
Envisioning New Ecosystems: A Conversation with Stewart Hoyt
Holding Space to Heal: A Conversation with Holly Ramey
Nature Sanctuary for the Future: A Conversation with Marina Levitina
What Art Can Do: A Conversation with Janet Morgan

Visit www.majesticwisdompublishing.com to learn more.